Baby Polar Bears at the Zoo

Cecelia H. Brannon

Enslow Publishing
101 W. 23rd Street
Suite 240
New York, NY 10011
USA
enslow.com

Published in 2016 by Enslow Publishing, LLC.
101 W. 23rd Street, Suite 240, New York, NY 10011

Library of Congress Cataloging-in-Publication Data

Brannon, Cecelia H.
  Baby polar bears at the zoo / by Cecelia H. Brannon.
     p. cm. — (All about baby zoo animals)
  Includes bibliographical references and index.
  ISBN 978-0-7660-7156-8 (library binding)
  ISBN 978-0-7660-7154-4 (pbk.)
  ISBN 978-0-7660-7155-1 (6-pack)
  1. Polar bear — Infancy — Juvenile literature. 2. Zoo animals — Juvenile literature. I. Brannon, Cecelia H. II. Title.
  QL737.C27 B73 2016
  599.786'139—d23

Printed in the United States of America

To Our Readers: We have done our best to make sure all website addresses in this book were active and appropriate when we went to press. However, the author and the publisher have no control over and assume no liability for the material available on those websites or on any websites they may link to. Any comments or suggestions can be sent by e-mail to customerservice@enslow.com.

Photos Credits: Cover, p. 12 olga_gl/Shutterstock.com; p. 1 Igor Kovalchuk/Shutterstock.com; pp. 4–5 Alexandr Junek Imaging s.r.o./Shutterstock.com; p. 6 © iStockphoto.com/Vassiliy Vishnevskiy; pp. 3 (left, center), 8, 10 marchello/Shutterstock.com; p. 14 © iStockphoto.com/Edoma; pp. 3 (right), 16 Fairfax Media/Getty Images; p. 18 Stayer/Shutterstock.com; p. 20 © iStockphoto.com/Enjoylife2; p. 22 bierchen/Shutterstock.com.

Contents

Words to Know

cub   fur   underwater

4

Who lives at the zoo?

A baby polar bear lives at the zoo!

A baby polar bear is called a cub.

A polar bear cub has white fur. But the skin underneath the white fur is black!

A polar bear cub loves to play. Playing helps it make friends with other cubs.

A polar bear cub loves to swim. Swimming keeps it cool and its fur clean.

A polar bear cub can see underwater. It has an extra clear eyelid that covers its eyes.

A polar bear cub eats meat and fish. It gets food from the zookeeper.

A polar bear cub lives in the zoo with its mother. The polar bear cub calls out to its mother by snorting.

You can see a polar bear cub at the zoo!

Read More

Josh, Gregory. *Polar Bears.* North Mankato, MN: Cherry Lake, 2012.

Marsh, Laura. *National Geographic Readers: Polar Bears.* Washington, DC: National Geographic Children's Books, 2013.

Websites

San Diego Zoo Kids: Polar Bear
kids.sandiegozoo.org/animals/mammals/polar-bear

National Geographic Kids: Polar Bear
kids.nationalgeographic.com/animals/polar-bear/

Index

Guided Reading Level: C
Guided Reading Leveling System is based on the guidelines recommended by Fountas and Pinnell.

Word Count: 130